AF472042

Best of William Knoblauch

Poetry and other

William Knoblauch

knoBBy
2015

First Printing: 2015

ISBN 978-1-329-15685-2

Knobby .inc
412 S. Vandiver Rd
San Antonio, TX 78209

www.AmericanFlat6.com

Best of William Knoblauch

Acknowledgements

I would like to thank my teacher, my writing classmates, and my family without whose help this book would never have been completed. You have helped me make this book and change the mistakes, you've told me what was good and bad.

Thank you for your patience and guidance, this book could not have been done.

Introduction

This is a book of poetry, not a novel. Don't think it's a novel, it's not. It is a book of poetry... At first then there are two shortstories just before the last poem. ***This is how I talk to you if I need to, just in case you were wondering.***

You're Not Looking

When looking
through a pond.
What you see
is only on the surface.
To see the
deeper parts of it,
you must enter the water.
Looking with
your mind.
But if you realize,
the pond,
is actually a lake.
You're not seeing.
You're not looking.

The Dome Will Live On

The dome,
the cover from society,
it judges.

You make
decisions
and it pushes you
this way and that.

But we don't
fight it.
We roll over
to show our
bellies.

But every one
in a million
fight.

Fight the dome,
watch it burn.

You have the power,
within you.

Every one does,
but no one knows.

And when you
fight,
for freedom
over the dome.

But the dome will
always be.

You can only
destroy it for
yourself.

You can help
others concur it,
but they have to
find it within them.
You can't win
the war
only the battles.

And
the dome will live on.

My Genius

Smooth lines with a salty texture,
hand crafted with paint and paper,
the two p's of art,
with only one purpose,
to show my genius.

Full of life,
but soulless.
Black and white
but full of colour.

My genius.
Only one person
can have it,
not you,
not them,
me.

Every once in a while,
one person,
with their eyes open,
and their judging glands closed,
will notice
my genius.

Some people say
a picture has a thousand words,

but a painting,
has millions.

Not all paintings
are made equal,
salty or not,
it does not matter,
but to show,
my genius.

Red and Pink

Silky smooth,
as if from
heaven.
Gift from
God,
nothing can
compare.
Like a
flower,
amongst all
others.
Red and pink,
with curves and
edges.
Like a
child,
someone will
find it.

Will You?

If I
make a
painting,
all salty and swift,
that shows all emotion,
and speaks in whispers
will you
hang it?

If I
write a short story,
with characterization
and
will you read it?

If I
make a great beat,
that sweeps the streets
will you
listen?

If I
make a cream pie,
that catches some eyes

and has a 20 person line
will you
eat it?

If I
make an equation,
that stuns
the world
will you
shun me and frown?

If I
make a moon base,
with O2 and H2O
and tons of space
will you
move there?

If I
make this my poem,
all silky and smooth
and hold it up high
will you
reach it,
or
will you
not try?

This next one is my favorite short story because of the ending…

Panton

"Should we do this?" I said .

"Yes, yes we need to do this." said Panton, while we walked up the hill as the sky became pure black with a beautiful array of stars. There was just a little dew on the grass. There was a tower on the hill and our spy's say it has a load of weapons, which should give us an upper hand against the mafia. Panton walked like he was about to die. We jumped down to the ground and lied down trying to avoid being seen by a car passing by.

"Three men" said Panton as The car came to a halt and I could smell the men from where I was.

"They must have saw us." I whispered. We sat there for a second until the car started moving again, but we didn't get up immediately, we learned that from experience. We started to crawl up the hill. When we almost got to the top, we heard some talking.

"Sounds like guards," Panton said "I'm gonna check." He lifted himself up over the crest in the hill. "Two guards. One has a assault rifle and the other a pistol. The one with the rifle has a grenade and a medical kit on his belt. The other has a holstered knife. They are talking about. Uhh."

He looked back at me. His eyes were completely blood shot. Panton has the eyes of a killer. He's seen death so much it's not even effecting his mood any more. I am completely the opposite. He looked at the guards again and began talking again.

"They are talking about the fire. Yeah, the fire that has been sweeping across the island."

"I miss Jason.", I said staring at the slippery grass.

"What?", said Panton .

"I... miss... Jason."

"Yeah, me too. Okay let's move up."

"You remember when he got that CD from the FBI and was almost arrested?", I said.

"Yeah whatever.", We walked in a circle around the fence that was around the guards. We got to a spot behind the fence with the guards on the other side. Panton pulled out a pistol with a silencer, he looked like he was caring for a baby.

"Wow, where did you get that."

"Found it on a body when I went out hunting.", whispered Panton. He aimed the weapon at the guard on the left and fired. Quickly he aimed at the other and fired. Neither of them knew what hit them.

We walked back around the fence and squished through the hole. Right then a truck with 5 guys pulled up. We looked back and saw them coming so we started to run. We walked up to the tower the guards had been guarding. Right as we opened the door a hand grabbed my shoulder. There was a tingling sensation of a needle entering my arm as I passed out.

While regaining consciousness I saw Panton standing there words were coming out of his mouth I just could not focus on them.

"Panton?" I said scanning the dark room. There a light above me, like in a movie. One guard on the left and another on the right.

"Yes! Yes! Yes! Yes! Finally you are awake, I mean I thought big boy over hear over dosed you! But no he didn't, and if he did I would kill him! Right?" said Panton.

"Ya boss, sorry." said big boy as he shrugged and turned his sweaty neck around.

"Okay now why do you think your here?"

"I don't know." I said half unconscious.

"Well you are the leader of the resistances and I'm the leader of the mafia."

"No your not."

"Actually I was the head of the resistance for a month now, since the boss died. I just was pretending. It was all an act! Now I'm gonna take you out, 'cause your in my way!"

To Be Continued

This next story is a little gorry and you can skip it if you like, but the twist is crazy.

His New Wife

It's 1982, the world has been totally robotized. Hitler has been molded with a robot and is the ruler of the world. We have found aliens on Mars and made them our allies. A colony on Mars has rebelled against Hitler and now fly space is restricted for "educational purposes". George and his wife Penny are normal people living in the world capital in Germany. Their house is protected by a Z0id shield, it has a shed where George works on his trains. The Z0id company has made all the electronics for the world. George and Penny sit on their couch, working on their holographic Z0id phones.

"Dang it Penny why didn't you tell me I had a dentist appointment at three today?"

"Sorry I forget things sometimes, and don't yell so loud, you know I have my Z0id hearing aid in for my hearing loss." said Penny poking her ear.

"Oh sorry Darling." whispered George.

"Let's watch TV" said Penny pointing at their Z0id Television.

"On that old thing."

"Yeah it'll be just like thirty years ago, when we would watch TV on the actual Television." she said looking up at the Television.

"Okay, you crazy lady." George said standing up,"I'm gonna grab a beer." he said walking to the kitchen. He opened the fridge and a huge blast of warm air hit him in the face.

"Honey the Z0id fridge is acting up again."

"Okay I'll call the repair bot to come and fix it." said Penny turning the volume of her hearing aid down. George then walked over to the wall computer and bought a beer. Lots of noise came from the pipes in the walls, a small opening appeared in the wall and a bud wëíser was sitting there. George got the beer and walked back to the living room and sat on the couch. The Television was on the news channel.

"Thank you Rob, this is Hillary and I am in neu new York where a robot has gone rouge, his cereal number is 456J0N4TH4N495 or Jonathan by local robots. He said 'I am the ruler, kill all humans.' and then a person ran up and stabbed him directly in the fuel pump. He fell over and leaked oil just right over here. He can shape shift which makes him extremely dangerous. Be careful. Now back to you Rob." George finished his beer and said, " I'm going to the shed." as he got up and walked out the back door. When he got out side he could smell motor oil, but he didn't think much of it. He walked over to the wooden shed and opened the door.

Just then the news channel went haywire to get back to Hillary. "We now have news from the airport that the rouge robot has just got on a plane for the world capital, everyone in the world capital should turn on their Z0id shield and stay put we will have coverage in a minute."

"George! George!" Penny screamed from in the house. The house had their Z0id shield already on because they turned out on the last day because a Mars attack was coming, but Penny forgot to turn it off. All Z0id shields make it to where you couldn't hear anything that happens inside so George didn't hear a thing.

As George was in the shed tinkering with his model trains, 456J0N4TH4N495 broke the wall furthest from the house. Jonathan kicked over the table and a train flew and hit George's knee. George feel over in pain. Jonathan took a transfer with the sharpest edge and stabbed George several times. George was bleeding really bad now. Jonathan waited him out, waiting for him to bleed to death. He took George and buried his body under the shed, then he fixed the wall he had broke. He then activated his shape shifting modal and turned into George. After changing he went inside to meet his new wife.

Table Salt

Salt on
my table,
changes in to
everything.
It is a
shape shifter
who has every
right to change
in to anything.

But you
must change
first.
You must make
the first move,
the first swipe
from the
motion of your
hand, moving the salt.

The salt on
my table,
it can be many things.
But I must change.

During the Fact

To set
you free,
complete a
task.
Look within
yourself, within
your soul.

Change
the perspective,
empty or full,
neither is
not the answer.

Neither is not a
solution to all
life long tails.
Life long stories.

This is just
the beginning

to set you free,
this is during the fact
not after.

Every thought

Every thought,
thought by every man
is a thought to keep.
Every single idea,
so different
from the rest.

So un touched by the
fatal hand of the populous.
Most of, have never
seen the
fabric of space,
never to come to life.

None of which have a
beginning or end.

People say
when you have
a good thought
write it down,
I say don't,
keep thinking of
that single thought
until it is so original
if anyone had the same
thought,
it would be

different.

But maybe difference
is bad,
a bad change,
but it makes
originality.

With everything
so different
there would be no
fight for the top,
and no fight means
no goals,
and no goals means
no thoughts,
and with no thought
we would do mindless
tasks.

Every thought
thought by every man
is different and the same.

This next poem is mostly talking to you and about you. It is interactive so to speak.

Flying

When falling through
your life,
do you see good or bad,
maybe both.

There is no
correct answer
because you don't
fall through your life
you

fly through.
Flying higher and faster
than everyone,
you explode.
Your life is chaos
when flying,
then why don't you

walk?
Is that better,
walking through
your life,
you think it is.
It wasn't like flying
but you'll get there
someday.

Now we are running,
running feels good,
but flying didn't get
you tired,
so

jog.
No one will judge you
on how slow
you're going,
this is your life,
your world.
As much as I have
said this flying was better.
lets

fly again.
Wow this is better,
flying.

Language

Emotion is
the language
for me.
The language
for all.

I know you
might use English,
but you cant show
what your thinking.

You might use Chinese,
the language of the
ninja masters,
but they don't show
emotion.

You might use Spanish,
the most slang language,
the language of emotion
has no slang.

You might use French,
the language of love,
but can you show if you're
happy or sad?

You might use emojis

for all I care,
it doesn’t match emotion.

But for now I
use English,
it’s nothing special
just combined
symbols to form words.

Dogs use the language
of emotion,
and look where
that’s got them.

Glossary

as·so·ci·a·tion (ə-sō′sē-ā′shən, -shē-)
n.
1. The act of associating or the state of being associated.
2. An organized body of people who have an interest, activity, or purpose in common; a society.
3.
a. A mental connection or relation between thoughts, feelings, ideas, or sensations.
b. A remembered or imagined feeling, emotion, idea, or sensation linked to a person, object, or idea.
4. A correlation or causal connection: *the association of exercise with improved sleep.*
5. *Chemistry* Any of various processes of combination, such as hydration, solvation, or complex-ion formation, depending on relatively weak chemical bonding.
6. *Ecology* A large number of organisms in a specific geographic area constituting a community with one or two dominant species.

loft (lôft, lŏft)
n.
1.
a. A large, usually unpartitioned floor over a factory, warehouse, or other commercial or industrial space.
b. Such a floor converted into an apartment or artist's studio.
2. An open space under a roof; an attic or garret.
3. A gallery or balcony, as in a church.
4. A hayloft.
5. *Sports*
a. The backward slant of the face of a golf club head, designed to drive the ball up off the ground.
b. A golf stroke that drives the ball in a high arc.
c. The upward course of a ball driven in a high arc.
6.
a. The thickness of a fabric or yarn.

b. The thickness of an item, such as a down comforter, that is filled with compressible insulating material.

dat·ed (dā′tĭd)
adj.
1. Marked with or displaying a date.
2. Old-fashioned; out-of-date.

puck (pŭk)
n.
A hard rubber disk used in ice hockey.

sty·lus (stī′ləs)
n. pl. **sty·lus·es** or **sty·li** (-lī)
1. A sharp, pointed instrument used for writing, marking, or engraving.
2. *Computers* A pointed instrument used as an input device on a pressure-sensitive screen.
3. A phonograph needle.
4. A sharp, pointed tool used for cutting the jagged grooves that record sound on a phonograph record.

www.ingramcontent.com/pod-product-compliance
Ingram Content Group UK Ltd.
Pitfield, Milton Keynes, MK11 3LW, UK
UKHW041901190726
13854UKWH00003B/1012

9 781329 156852